CW01663217

Life As I See It

To Jean

Life As I See It

Gwyneth Cleworth

Best Wishes

Gwyneth Cleworth.

Heron's View Publications

First published in 2004 by
Heron's View Publications
281 Chorley New Road,
Bolton BL1 4PH

© Gwyneth Cleworth 2004
illustrations © the respective illustrators

ISBN 0 9546734 0 9 *paperback*

The right of Gwyneth Cleworth to be identified as the author of this work has been asserted by her in accordance with the Copyright, Design and Patents Act 1988.

All rights reserved. No part of this publication may be reproduced in any material form (including photocopying or storing it in any medium by electronic means and whether or not transiently or incidentally to some other use of publication) without the written permission of the copyright owner except in accordance with the provisions of the Copyright, Designs and Patents Act 1988 or under the terms of a licence issued by the Copyright Licensing Agency Ltd. 90 Tottenham Court Road, London, England W1P 9HE. Applications for the copyright owner's written permission to reproduce any part of this publication should be addressed to the publisher.

Produced by Freelance Publishing Services,
Brinscall, Lancs
www.freelancepublishingservices.co.uk
Printed in Great Britain by Antony Rowe Ltd,
Eastbourne

Contents

Foreword

Gwyneth Cleworth is a pleasant, active lady who I have known for a good many years. She is of enquiring mind and her thoughts are on life and on the living of life. Thoughts which she presents through her love of writing.

She is a poetess with a common touch whose words encapsulate the patterns of life that surround her. Her work is easy to read, is uplifting to all levels of intelligence and it provides the reader with that warm inner feeling that denotes the spending of a pleasant and worthwhile hour of one's time.

I have no hesitation in recommending her poetry to each and every one. Sit back, relax, and enjoy Gwyneth's work, NAY! not work, her labour of love! Your time will be well spent, I assure you!

Brian Clare
Dialect poet and raconteur
October 2003

About the author

I was born in Bolton, my maiden name being Gwyneth Heron. Then we went to live in the south of England. I remember going to Yardley Lane Primary School, Chingford, Essex, when I was five years of age. The Second World War started and by then we had moved to Ilford. I was evacuated to a small Bedfordshire village and later to Bolton to live with my grandparents. I attended St Matthew's Primary School and then Canon Slade Grammar School.

By this time I had two brothers and one sister. I married Graham Cleworth in 1955, then had two daughters and one son. After twenty years working in Local Govenment at Bolton Town Hall, Planning Department, I am retired. Now I have six grandchildren to add to my pleasure, often featuring in my poems.

Life as I see it has inspired me to write poetry. I have seen many changes in our world and my observations are reflected in poems. I have been writing for at least twenty years, with my work appearing in many anthologies. The jobs I had before Local Government have also enriched my life; working for a solicitors and as a doctor's receptionist. All these etched into my memory, which I now share with you.

Gwyneth Cleworth
November 2003

Acknowledgements

I would like to thank most sincerely my husband Graham and all my family and friends for supporting my poetic venture, also Brian Clare for his Foreword.

I must also thank the *Bolton Evening News* for printing many of my poems in their 'Poets' Corner', hence furthering my interest.

My sincere thanks for the illustrations to:

my grandson Matthew Booth (10 years of age), for those on pages 1 and 19;

my good friends: Mr Tom Newton MBE, Westhoughton comedian and artist, for those on pages 7, 9, 18, 29, 47, 58, 61, 81 and 82;

and Mr Ross Mills, portraits and fine artist (www. mills-art.com), for those on pages 16, 52, 67, 71, 79 and 89.

Evacuate

During World War II I was evacuated from William Talbot School, Ilford, to a village in Bedfordshire. I was seven years old – not a very happy time in my life.

During the war, I remember so well
Although many long years have now gone
I was seven and scared, seven and scarred
Those memories a cloak I must don.

Evacuate, evacuate, the words shouted at me
Gathered together and wrenched from our
   homes.
Packed, then labelled, sent out of the way
A wall of us stacked like stones.

The station, then train, goodbyes and tears.
Forced camaraderie, sweets to help the bitter
   taste.
The whistle, the unknown, unfriendly faces
Regardless the carrier of fear sped with haste.

To where and to who, what fate for me
To sit in a school room and wait.
My name at last – to the door I was led.
Like a puppy I was chosen, the rest – just hate.

Look Alike Dream

When she was just a little girl
Shirley Temple was all the rage.
How she yearned and envied her,
Wishing she was on the stage.

Her hair was straight and straggly
Not a wave or a curl in sight.
She thought her mother could put things
right.
She tried that very night!

Pipe cleaner curlers, oh so many
Were screwed into her hair.
She winced each turn, but persevered,
For tomorrow she'd be there.

She dreamed of a Shirley look alike,
And tossed and turned all night.
Desperate to get the curlers out.
Good Heavens – what a fright!

Her mother tried to convince her,
She swore she was Shirley's double.
But the mirror quickly told her
And sadly burst her bubble.

So remember all would-be look alikes,
Disappointing though it seems.
It's only a game called 'wishing',
And there's nothing wrong with dreams.

Childhood Games

I like to remember our childhood games
When fantasy and fun had no equal.
Schoolyards and cobbled streets alike
Absorbed each generation sequel.

Where did they go? No trace to be found.
Were top and whip just dreams?
When the spinning tops whizzed with kalei-
doscope colours
Of blues and greens and creams.

The Top macadam was our playground
Surely designed with our interest at heart.
It was better than any smart film set
No props ever needed from the start.

The scene was transformed as with seasons
For the old games returned year by year.
With ropes, bats and balls and conkers
Each child tried his skills without fear.

We played Donkey, May I and Hopscotch
With Kick-out Ball a favourite with most.
But the fun we all had Truth or Daring
Gave many an excuse to boast.

We pestered our mums for old pram wheels
When racing trolleys were the vogue.
The skills and daring of budding speed kings
Fired ambition in many a rogue.

The Torvills and Deans of that day
Really gave our macadam some hammer.
Then quick change to Finger, Thumb or Icky –
Each exciting new games caused clamour.

There were May Queens and Ippy Chippy
  Charlies
You may well ask – Ippy Chippy Who?
Lads dressed in rags, danced round maypoles
With faces all blackened with soot.

Our joy was not measured with money
For life's real pleasures are free.
Those old games brought a wealth of friend-
  ship
With a treasure of memories for me.

Our Coalman

The harsh winter weather
Brought memories of old.
When a roaring coal fire
Was worth more than gold.

Jimmy was our coalman,
I remember him well,
With his coal dusty face,
'How many?' he'd yell.

The coal thundered in,
The bunker – soon full.
Jimmy counted the empties,
Midst dust cloud and lull.

Back to his wagon,
To heave once again.
His back must be breaking,
He doesn't complain.

His visits were welcome.
When embers were low.

The coal Jimmy brought us,
Rekindled our glow.

The fireside is changed.
Now Jimmy's gone.
We've accepted the new,
But memory plods on.

A Lancashire life character,
Who soon proved his worth,
Our coalman called Jimmy,
The salt of the earth.

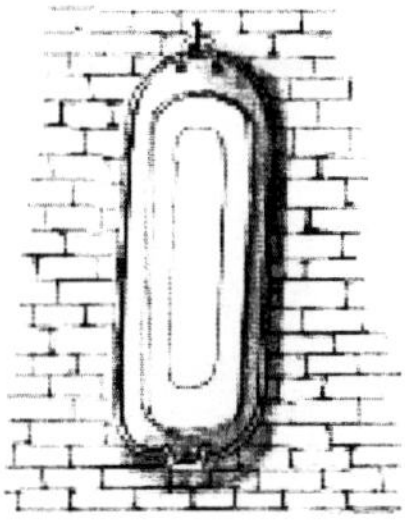

The Old Tin Bath

The old tin bath,
I remember so well,
Hanging on the back yard wall.
Every Friday night,
It was lifted down,
Then each one, in turn
Shed all.
Soap and towel,
Clean nightwear,
Were ready as the bath was filled.
Jug by jug, all clean and fresh,
Not a drop of water was spilled.
The first one in,
Had to make it brief,
Clean water was luxury enough!
The next one in,
Had the water cooled down,
And the next and the next had it rough.
For the last in the bath it was a downright
shame,
As no one could be more unlucky,
Than to sit in a bath,
With its secrets held fast,
And the cold water now turned mucky!

Our streets held many memories for us. It's sad to see the houses demolished. Not much money but a wealth of friendliness. Help if you needed it, no locked doors, a safer world.

Demolition

The street is dying,
Few houses remain.
Huddled, barely lit,
Shrouded with rain.

The street was alive,
Not too long ago.
Where have they gone,
Those who would know?

Like an illness it crept,
The dank and disease.
Eased out all the neighbours,
Leaving hollows – no breeze.

Laughter once reigned,
In this well loved street.
Now only echoes still haunt,
Where once there were feet.

Begone street, make way
For all that is new.
But lock up your memories,
They are only for you.

If Only I'd Listened

If only I'd listened to mi Mam and Dad,
And got mi head down at school.
They said I'd be sorry, and now I've found
out.
If only I'd listened and not been a fool.

I didn't believe them, how right they were,
You don't realise when you're a kid,
It's your world and your mates that matter
then,
Your future always stays well hid.

Time after time mi Mam and Dad went on.
They dreamed of something better for their
brood.
Knowing too well the hard times,
Hardly enough money for food.

They gave me the opportunity,
I should have grasped it with both hands.
Play, play, play, but never work,
I chose to ignore all their demands.

They said this day would surely come,
And I know exactly what they meant,
But if only I'd listened to mi Mam and Dad,
I might not regret those school days spent.

With three of mi own, now history repeats.
What a job mi Mam and Dad must have had!
I can only hope, mine won't be like me,
Wishing they'd listened to their Mam and
  Dad.

Where Did It All Go?

Where did it all go,
Did I just blink? – time flies,
It can't all have gone, so soon,
Let me rub my eyes.

A little girl at school,
With Mum, Dad and more kids,
The war – then split, make way,
While life trickles down the grids.

Disappearing friends and kin,
In a world of shifting sand,
My special Gran and Grandad,
There was talk of a better land.

School and boyfriends,
Then jobs and so much fun,
And days didn't ever matter,
There was always another one.

It's a different way of life now,
But I never saw it change,

No TV, video or micro-chips,
All these things would be strange.

Marriage vows and babies three,
Seems only a day or two,
Now they're grown-up and left us,
As we brought them up to do.

But life's so short or so it seems,
An afforded glimpse to treasure,
I wish I'd savoured each precious moment,
And drunk of life's full measure.

Where did it all go?
And friends and kin I knew.
I'll never know the answer,
And neither, dear reader, will you!

My Father

There he sits in his ultra-bright room.
Chromium taps, shining floor.
He has a view of lawns,
Where he will walk no more.
He nods in recognition at loving nurses, but not me.
Frozen that day and not even reached his Autumn.
He has time to reflect but not undo.
How can he be happy?
He is comfortable and cared for too,
But no – not happy.

We're Off

We are packing for our holiday
A happy family chore.
Thank goodness it's an annual event
I can't stand any more.

Squashing, cramming, sitting, jamming
How will it all fit in?
Surely we can't need all this stuff
There isn't room for a pin.

Oh yes, everything now packed in tight
What a treat in store.
Has no one seen the keys for the case?
No, not the panic once more!

Off with the electric, water, gas
Everything going smooth
We've only to check that doors are locked
Then we are ready to move.

The next step seems quite easy,
To the airport, driven by a friend

Scurrying traffic, lights always red
Will this journey never end?

Well, we have made it to the airport
Waved goodbye to our chauffeur
Once more, search for tickets
Now spot the seasoned traveller.

Now we are queuing for the Customs,
   Passports clutched in our hands.
Good Heavens, what's all the clanging?
It sounds like the great massed bands.

It's only the detector detecting
Recording its find on Dad.
A pair of glasses causes all that fuss,
The biggest fright he's had.

Our holiday start is an assault course
With a seat on the plane as a prize.
At last all the family have qualified,
A reward for each one who tries.

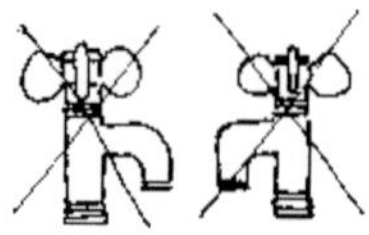

Nae Water

Our holiday could have been a disaster. There really was 'nae water' for a few days. Even the swimming pool was empty. We made the best of it, met some great people including the staff. A happy ending.

Ah, Portugal, our choice this year.
Fun and sun and atmosphere.
Holiday revellers, a good crowd were we.
Hotel should be good, with star rating three.

Alas, dismay, as we arrived in the dark.
Stunned silence then as we slowly embarked.
We couldn't believe that the plank was for us.
First thoughts for all 'Get back on the bus!'

However, we were tired, we'd give them a chance,
A miracle was needed, we could see at a glance.
With shower, drink and a good night's rest,
We could face all problems with renewed zest.

Did I say shower? Well that was a laugh.
Nor did we get a much needed bath.
For there was 'Nae Water', as our Scots friends declared,
Unless you were a plant – then no water spared!

The plants shot up overnight – six foot high,
Leaving us poor holidaymakers shrivelled and dry.
Like the pub with no beer, that was our luck at first.
No way to wash or even quench our thirst.

The UK Rep and British Consul came too.
From Lisbon he sped to see what was to do.
'There's Nae Water you see', our Scots friends soon told.
We now realised it was worth more than gold!

We're on the best building site – Wimpey would be proud.
We weren't impressed, and told them so – loud.
Our holiday hotel was real Scottish mist,
Nae Water, three stars and a tale with a twist.

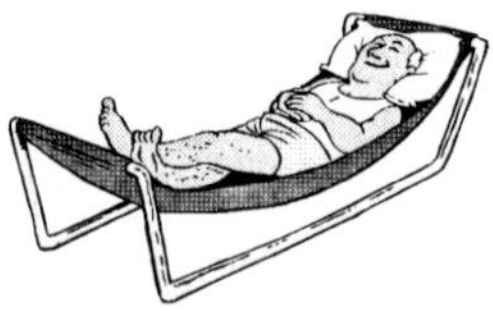

Browned Off

Pasty faces, pasty bodies,
Pasty feet and hands.
Only changing colours,
When we visit foreign lands.

Weary flagging footsteps,
Creaking joints and bones,
Tired of watching TV
Where, not only sheep are clones.

We'll soon be on the suncream slide,
And turning as if on a grill.
Changing colour from lobster to puce,
Until we've had our fill.

'What a lovely tan you've got',
As from holiday we return.
'Yes, I soon turn brown – no problem',
Forgetting those third degree burns!

'It's been scorching while you've been away,
But there's bad weather ahead, we're told.'

If my tan turns to rust – I'll still sport it.
Believe me, I'm definitely going for gold!

I jest of course, and know,
True colour shines from within.
A healthy glow, or pasty face,
Who cares about colour of skin?

Cruising

Now, our last holiday,
Was really the best.
Cruising in the Caribbean,
It put all others to the test.

Such beautiful islands,
Sunshine, sea and sand,
And swaying palms say Welcome,
To music of calypso bands.

As they greet you in their islands,
The locals are top of the pops.
Their happy smiling faces,
Match the jewels in their shops.

Life on board ship,
Believe me was great,
Service reached perfection, and
Enhanced the food we ate.

But talking about food,
That really is another mattter.

It's a wonder we didn't sink,
With everyone ending up fatter!

A weightwatcher's nightmare!
With wallets thin and people fat.
Caribbean cruising,
Is it worth all that?

But we went with good friends,
And met many more,
Yes, that's what really matters,
Afloat or shore!

Holiday Packing

There was many a time,
Long long ago,
When off on holiday I went,
Not a care in the world,
Just pack up and go,
Till all my money was spent.

Did I pack any tablets,
Potions or pills?
Never did such things cross my mind!
Make-up and curlers, earrings and such,
But nothing of a medical kind.

How things have changed, since those days,
It's a fully equipped ambulance I need now,
Or at least a travelling chemist
And books packed with hints and know how.

I have midge bites and earache,
To cope with,
Pills for starting and stopping,
Not to mention heatstroke and blisters galore,

I need a full day for medical shopping!

At the Customs I was even asked,
Was I going on a medical course?
They hoped that I passed with honours,
Little knowing these things were enforced!

It's part of the ageing process,
Or I'm cracking up real fast.
Don't think it's only me needs these pills,
There's none of us here built to last!

Dumpling and Stew

Have you heard of those two kittens?
One called Dumpling, the other Stew?
The cutest little felines
Who cause such a hullabaloo.
The other morn, just after dawn
Their owners rushed around.
They aimed to get to work on time –
Too much to ask, they found.
Dumpling and Stew had different plans
As they darted to and fro.
A pan of porridge filled to the brim
Was featured in their show.
Surprised how far the porridge spread
Their owners counted ten
As they slipped and trod upon those kits
And trod and slipped again.
So morning turned to bathtime
For cats and owners too.
You'll see them hanging out to dry
Little Dumpling and sister Stew.

Doggone

We once had a dog called Bobbie,
He was supposed to be part Great Dane,
The biggest part, I venture to add,
And a challenge for all to train …

But train him we did, in a fashion,
His 'walkies' made interesting feats.
Comparisons with 'Boy on a Dolphin',
Were often the neighbourhood treats.

Sometimes if the weather turned nasty,
Our Bobby still went out for jogs,
He kept pace with the flow of the slow
 stream,
The envy of all other dogs.

The idea was for us to keep dry,
Whilst still giving our pet a treat,
So we drove the car with great caution,
And Bobbie did the trip on four feet!

His lolloping gait was endearing,
And his appearance a pill in reverse,
All sweetness and honey inside, but
When angry he couldn't look worse.

His appetite was insatiable,
An obsession – or so it seemed.
He thoroughly enjoyed his minced mortals,
I'm sure food featured high in his dreams.

The supermarket shelves were soon emptied,
As we bought lots of food for our Bob,
We were farming him out for two weeks,
So we really did do a good job!

But sadly that's when it happened,
Bobby got wind of things brewing,
He decided he'd hop it for ever,
And left us all worrying and stewing.

We searched high and low and did adverts,
He just disappeared without trace.
Bad enough him just leaving in that way,
It's the mountain of food we can't face!

Endangered Species

Giant Pandas, resplendent in black and white.
Such a delight to behold.
Their rare offspring, so engaging and cute.
These babies are worth more than gold.

There are probably more in captivity now,
Beautiful animals and not many left.
Tragic if they disappeared from our world.
Leaving memories, and us, sadly bereft.

With a staple diet of bamboo shoots,
Their demands are very few.
They seem so shy and appealing,
I hope they never vanish – don't you?

The natural disasters which occur in our world such as earthquakes, famine, floods and drought, are beyond the control of man. I write about these terrible things and my heart goes out to the victims. But environmental disasters are men's dong and must be halted before it's too late. Hence my poem: Earth Matters.

Earth Matters

Do you still want,
All your Jacks and Jills,
To wander and play,
On lush green hills?

Do you want them to drink,
The waters, so clear,
And fill up their lungs,
For many a year.

With clean fresh air,
Their right – from birth?
Then please protect,
Our gift of earth.

Its yield is unfailing,
We reap with joy,
Whilst man can build,
So can man destroy.

Our air is polluted,
And rivers and seas,

Feed death and destruction,
To livestock and trees.

Chemicals forge the link,
In every known guise,
From the depths of the oceans,
To the acid rain skies.

Let's not leave a legacy,
Of barren decay,
Earth matters for our children's
Tomorrows today!

Baby Boom

Have you noticed there is a Baby Boom?
Well, amongst my colleagues there is
It's more like a mass invasion,
Than a casual Master or Miss.

There's Beccie, Christopher and Ben,
And Baby Louise to name four,
Just as I write we have Matthew,
And I've just heard there's soon to be more.

It's wonderful news we keep hearing,
The population explosion is here,
And as for these bonnie babies,
They're top of the pops – that's clear.

We're delighted to see these offspring,
Complete with Mum and Dad,
Their cooing and gooing is enchanting,
To see peace reign makes us feel glad.

Then all of a sudden, without warning,
They size up the scene with a glance,

Talk about quick change artists,
Supply food – it's your only chance!

Now the smiles and pleasantries dispensed
with,
Making way for yells, screams and tears,
Time to say 'Cheerio, Mum and Dad,
Off you go with your little dears'.

And as I said in the beginning,
This baby thing has really caught on.
Well, here's to the next and the next,
They've started – so let them go on!

Please Mam

'Mam, can I go out and play?'
'Not till you've finished your tea.'
'Mam, please can I go out to play,
My mates are waiting for me?'

'Mam, I don't feel very hungry,
We had a big dinner at school.'
'I'm telling you lad, you're not going out,
Do you think your Mam's a fool?'

'I've never liked greens and all that stuff,
In fact I feel quite ill.'
'In that case, I'll send your mates packing,
And you up to bed with a pill!'

'I feel very much better now, Mam,
I can see that greens do you good.
Can I go out and play now, Mam?
I've just finished my very last spud.'

Grandsons

Two little grandsons,
Devils in disguise.
Eyes that speak volumes,
As they cajole and entice.

Yes it's all a ploy,
Just wait and you'll see.
'Little darlings, bless them,
Of course bring them to tea'.

We all make mistakes,
They're only one and six,
One's sat in the dog's water,
The other's gone finding sticks.

Grandad yanks him in,
We clear up the floor,
One's now glued to the telly,
I'm sure the other one swore!

Oh, visitors are here,
Show them how clever you are.

They've never done that before!
They'd make Noel Edmonds see stars!

They're just showing off,
All children do it.
Energy builds up,
Oh dear, they just blew it!

Now it's time to eat,
This should be great,
Hide the ketchup and pickles,
Put that back on the plate!

I now know why,
Chocolate spread gets its name,
One table, two faces,
And the dog gets the blame!

In fact the dog's getting fat,
He thinks the floor's a large plate,
As he dashes to relish,
These treats from his mates.

Now it's bath, nappy, and bottle.
Gosh, this really takes us back.
Bedtime stories last for ever,
As they bring books by the sack!

We love it really, you've guessed,
As they curl up to sleep.
Little darlings – bless them,
I'll just take another peep!

Their First Spring

Two new grandaughters
On the threshold of their world.
What beautiful sights to greet them,
As Earth's pages are unfurled.

Their first Spring, will create memories,
As they are introduced to its splendour.
With the blossom, flowers and lush greens,
Like all babies, new, delightful and tender.

But wait a moment, their *first* Spring!
Will it always be this way,
Or could things go wrong, and change,
Could this really happen one day?

We are often told, 'Protect our earth',
By those who really care.
And if we don't, who takes the blame,
Leaving no earthly dreams to share?

And as our grandaughters greet,
The arrival of their first Spring,
We hope it is followed by many,
Full of the happiness, our Earth can bring.

Bedtime Worry

Were you ever frightened of the dark,
  Grandma,
And lightning and thunder?
Did the shadows in your room jump out,
And the bed have creatures under?

Did you listen to funny noises, Grandad,
Real scary in the night?
When your Mum and Dad had gone to bed,
And there wasn't any light.

Will you hold my hand tonight, Grandma,
While Grandad looks around,
And can I stay downstairs tonight,
Until the monster's found?

I *know* there are no monsters,
It's really all pretend,
But just stay by my side tonight,
And I'll *always* be your friend.

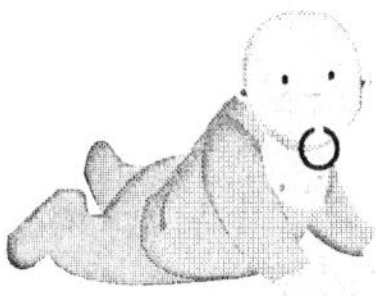

(Bolton Evening News) *Bonny Babies*

Bonny babies by the score,
Page after page.
Then even more!
Little boys, little girls,
Some no hair, some with curls.
Toothy grins, some smile bowt!
Some looking tough,
With nowt taken out!
Beautiful frocks and suits too,
Cute hats and caps,
And a bow or two.
Every baby adored by family and friends,
Each one is gorgeous!
What a splendid trend,
A daunting task,
Who could possibly choose?
It knocks spots off the Lottery,
It could even blow a fuse.
Such a gathering of cute babies,
Bolton should be proud.
A Judges' nightmare,
What a beautiful crowd!

Every one is a winner,
Of that we're quite sure,
They must choose with a *pin*,
Oh look, here come more!
Judges need more time,
As the numbers increase,
For the longest running contest,
That never seems to cease!

Promises

What is a promise, Grandma?
Why must I always keep it?
And why must it never be broken,
Is it a bit like a secret?

A very important question,
We must be clear when we reply.
For our lives depend on promises,
How else would we survive?

Promises are made by everyone,
This happens all through life.
From the tiny babe in arms,
For some, between man and wife.

Men and women in high places,
World leaders fit the bill.
Torrents of promises fall on us all,
And often failure to fulfil.

We are promised a peaceful world,
'Ceasefire, ceasefire', we hear.
It's amazing how we believe this,
But a promise was made – quite clear.

And then the bombs and bullets again,
Disillusioned, we ask – why?
Can't men live side by side in peace,
Or at least give it a try?

Broken promises bring sadness,
No easy task to recover,
And the teachings of life's lessons,
Are ours to cruelly discover.

How do we get our seasons,
Which return year after year,
And the sun and rain, our lifeline?
Our Creator promised they would be here.

So when you're asked 'What is a promise?'
Your answer must truthfully explain,
It means you *will* do what you say,
And your efforts will not be in vain.

Snow Recovery

Do I 'ave to go to school, Mam?
I've got a cold and a cough and a chill!
It's snowing hard and piling up,
I can see it on the sill.

Do I 'ave to go to school, Mam?
I bet the bus won't even come.
It'll only make me worse, Mam,
If I only do one sum!

It's mi 'ead that aches a lot, Mam,
And the white snow hurts mi eyes.
It's better keeping warm, Mam,
I'll help you bake some pies?

Eh, our Jimmy's making snowballs,
And mi mates are sledgin' all over t' place!
I can see 'em all thru t' winder, Mam,
Now they're 'aving a race!

It's not good mollicoddlin' mi,
It's stuffy by this fire.

Some fresh air 'll do mi good, Mam,
I bet I can throw them higher!

I was just thinking about the snowballs, Mam,
The exercise and all that.
I'll have to rush fert bus, Mam,
Just wait – our Jimmy – take that!

Oh, Mam

Oh Mam, please let me stay up tonight
And watch the best on TV.
I'm the only lad in our class
Who's sent to bed after tea!

Oh Mam, go on, just this once please,
I'll wash all the pots and pans,
I'll even take the dog out
And not kick any cans.

Oh Mam, you're not even listening to me,
You're doing what you warn me about.
Why is mi dad coming for me?
Ouch! I didn't expect that clout.

I'm only asking nicely, Mam,
To stay up to watch the telly,
All my mates' dads let them,
They don't just put in the welly!

I've promised to do mi homework,
Put the top on the toothpaste and such.

I'm only asking for half an hour.
Mi mates don't do *so* much.

I'll probably end up by being a saint
With all this good stuff I keep doing!
Then you'll be sorry you said 'No' when I
  asked
For just a measly half hour viewing.

Mi Grandad

Mi Grandad's mostly good,
He picks me up from school,
But sometimes, when we're driving home,
He'll call someone a fool!

He says those words he shouldn't,
You've told him, not in front of me,
And what does taxidermist mean?
He said something about a tree!

He's a very friendly Grandad,
He waves a lot as he drives,
People sometimes wave back,
Shouting something about a bunch of fives!

It's just those words you've told him about,
I thought it only right you know.
And it's only when he's speeding,
And never when going slow!

He's very sporty, mi Grandad,
Watching football and rugby on TV,

He cheers like mad when his team scores,
But if they don't – it's not 'dearie me'!

He's back to using those words again,
An' 'ow he can do better himself.
The ref's playin' fert others and turning a
blind eye,
An' needs glasses from t' National 'Ealth!

It's best when we call at the toffee shop,
Oh, now the secret's out.
He said there's nowt wrong with his teeth,
He's had plenty of sweets – no doubt!

Grandma leaves him healthy food,
To try and get him slim,
But unknown to her, it's fish and chips
He gets – especially when I'm out with him!

He said it's OK breaking rules,
As he piles sugar in his tea.
But I'll never split on mi Grandad,
Because he's mostly good, like me!

Babysit

Here we are, hope you are going to be good boys. What do you mean, no! It's a good job you are only two years old, lad, or else! I'll let you off this time. Now, let's see, where is your big brother? Oh yes, I can hear him crashing about upstairs. OK, Mum and Dad, you two go off and have a nice meal, quick before the little one escapes – bye.

There's no sleep in these two yet, I can see we are going to be at it all night! All right, you can get the train set out for a little while. The train driver *did not say that,* it's a swear word. No, Grandad didn't say it either. Who said the driver's a pilchard Oh, Grandad? Your brother's gone very quiet – come downstairs, please. It's taking you a long time on that toilet. A plum stone! Surely you're not still looking for that. It was a week ago, what, Katie and Alison have been looking for it as well! Yes, I know Matthew swallowed 5p. No, you can't have it when we find it, we've stopped looking for it. Come on, you two, it's bathtime and you should be in bed by now anyway. Matthew, take that little ball out of your mouth now! Take it out of your ear! And away from your nose, all right – you can hold it near your neck, yes, under your chin. I really don't know why they make such dangerous toys! Close that fridge door, Daniel, what's that? You can have some wine because it says 'Serve child' on the label. *Chilled*, you mean, you silly lad! Bath, at once! See, Matthew has completely emptied the toilet roll now. He did the same thing in that hotel in Wales. I had to stuff miles of toilet paper in my handbag, otherwise they would have thought there was an outbreak of dysentry in the place. Dysentry – no it's not a swear word! Get on with it, that's right, wash everything – yes – everything! It's too late to be answering those kind of questions, your Mum and Dad will talk to you tomorrow – I'm fed up of hearing about Katie and Alison! What will your little brother think! No you don't stink Matthew, I said think. Right, into bed you two. Yes, I'll listen to you reading Daniel. That's very good, carry on, you've only read half a page – *No*, reading the wine bottle lable doesn't count! I'll just read a little story to Matthew. Then we'll say our prayers. *Prayers*, you don't have to go to church to say prayers! God listens all the time. Come on now, there's a good lad, you've nearly gone through the whole Toys R Us catalogue! You are not supposed to ask God for things just for yourself all the time! That's right, just mention your Mum, Dad and little brother as well. No Daniel, Katie and Alison won't want the plum stone when you find it! Yes, God does know where the plum stone is, yes, and the 5p that Matthew swallowed. Yes, Children in Need would be glad of it – just leave that one to God! I'm sure He'll know what to do. Goodnight, God Bless. Thank goodness for that, everything's gone quiet. Hi, you're soon back. Yes, they've been wonderful, bless them, no problem, any time.

Children in Need

Children in need, should never be.
We see them on TV.
Children are our most precious gift,
Bestowed on you and me.

It's heartbreaking when they suffer,
If we can help them beat their pain,
And meet their needs in any way,
To give, is the way to gain.

We may not bring great change,
But just light relief means so much.
And a smile will be reward enough,
Meaning 'Thank You', with a golden touch.

So, if you can help in any way,
To bring a sparkle to their eyes.
It's a way of saying 'Thank You' in return,
And give Children in Need a lovely surprise.

Innocent, Mi Lord

'Innocent, mi Lord.'
'And how old are you?'
'Just born today, mi Lord.'
'Ah – as pure as the morning dew.'

'If only you could stay that way,
Instead of tainted by life's wrongs.
How think your guardians, my child,
Do they know where love belongs?'

'All newly born are innocent,
till moulded by sculptors of life,
Some wonderful mentors bring riches,
But the evil ones bring strife.'

'Parents should be judged early,
Can they handle this precious charge,
Teach right from wrong by example,
And protect from the wicked at large?'

'How many parents or kin,
If I were to judge and ask,

How think you on this subject,
Are you prepared for this special task?'

'With such treasures in your care,
And a challenge that exceeds the sword,
Could you answer – as this tiny babe,
'Innocent, mi Lord.'

Abandoned Baby

I saw you this morning on TV
Along with millions I'm sure.
Your little tearstained face,
Just three months old, no more.

I prayed your Mum would see you,
If only for relief to know,
You are well cared for and loved,
Never really cast out – oh no.

It was an appeal to find your Mum,
To help her and give her support.
She must be missing you badly.
Giving you up, would be the last resort.

To abandon her precious baby girl,
Takes more courage filled with fear,
Than we can ever begin to imagine.
The thought brings many a tear.

Your Mum has all the answers,
As the questions crowd into her head.

If by chance, she saw you on TV,
I believe, by her heart, she'll be led.

To discover a world of kindness and forgiv-
ing,
Never a question raised about blame.
Just help plan her daughter's future,
And perhaps, to a listening world – explain.

Whichever way things develop,
One fact is certain you'll see.
You will be brought up by those who realise,
How special baby girls can be!

After this poem appeared in the *Bolton Evening News* I was invited to join them on their next trip to the seaside. It was an honour to be part of it. The children had a wonderful time.

Cavalcade to the Sea

I've just witnessed a splendid sight.
A mass exodus from Bolton Town.
Dozens of kind taxi-drivers,
Doing good deeds for which they're re-
  nowned.

It's an annual event undertaken,
Shared by children less fortunate than most.
Such deserving and grateful passengers,
Reward enough for their generous hosts.

I'm sure it will be smiles all the way.
On their happy journey to the sea,
As horns tooted on festooned vehicles,
Intoxicating their charges with glee.

They'll have a wonderful time in the sun-
  shine,
And something to remember this day.
Let's banish the dark deeds all around us, and
Thank our taxi-drivers, as they lead the way

Lourdes – 1995

Well it's that special time again,
That important time of the year.
When Harold, Colin and Father Jim,
Upsticks and disappear!

Along with many others, some strong,
Some gathering strength whilst on the way.
Such kind and caring people,
Will disperse any clouds of grey.

And who better to allay any fears,
Than Nurse Judith, with tender loving care.
A doctor on hand, with skills to be proud,
Such a blessing to see them there.

It's a laugh from beginning to end, I'm told.
Even the frail are renewed with vigour.
This is well before their destination is
reached,
And the carer's hearts grow bigger.

Yes, we know now, where they are going.
On a wonderful pilgrimage to Lourdes.

There will be ups and downs, along the way,
Of this they are assured.

But a happier crowd, you couldn't meet,
They are prepared for what's in store.
From the laughs and jokes, and singing too,
Father Christmas, fancy dress and more!

Some of those present, may enjoy a wee dram,
And some, may even relish two!
But when they have all had cold baths and
shivered,
They all turn the same shade of blue!

When they join long torchlight processions,
Paying homage, sharing prayers and hope,
And wondering if there are any miracles left,
Yet if not – just knowing they will cope.

Listen

Listen and hear – listen and learn.
A powerful gift, which takes our time.
The key to problems, needing our help,
Yet a blessing for those with mountains to
climb.

Too many complacent, too many don't care.
Dismissive, cocooned in their worlds.
If they could spare a minute, to listen, that's
all.
To those less fortunate, Lady Luck has
spurned.

Make life more bearable,
And help share the load.
Reap rewards without measure,
As we all travel the same road.

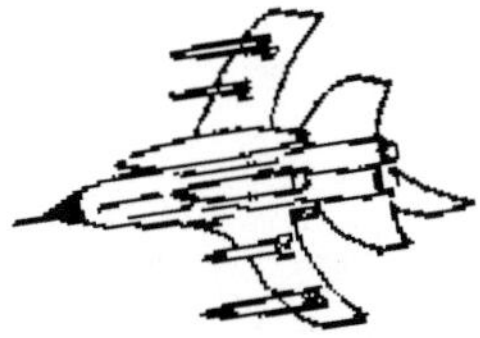

Keep Safe, My Child

My son's friend was a Tornado pilot during the Gulf War. I wrote this poem for his mum. He returned safely, I am happy to say.

'Please keep safe, my child',
Mothers whispered all over the world.
'Don't worry, Mum, only the good die young'.
And that cruel lesson we've learned.

'Come back soon, my child',
And their prayers were heard.
For most of them were spared, we know.
And yet, for some there's been no word.

Sadly, some fell on foreign soil,
Heroes, every inch of the way.
It's *their* mothers who whispered,
'Keep safe, my child',
Their mothers for whom we pray.

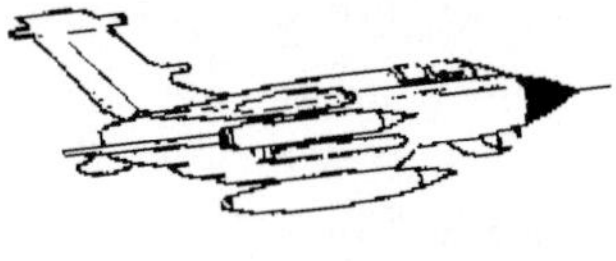

Life – No Re-run

I believe – we have one chance.
High or low birth, may decide
Whether we sink, or swim, or float through
  life.
As do the rules, by which we abide.

Life's journey may be re-traced, in the mind.
But never re-lived in the flesh.
So, a prophet is he who realises this,
And does not treat life as a jest.

Greed is often the cause of pain.
Trapping multitudes in its wake.
There is no re-run here, to make amends,
To heal and soothe the hearts that break.

Yet life is surely for living,
To enjoy and feast on its gifts.
Perhaps we are blind to its glory,
Swept by tides, which rage, then drift.

The only answer – look forward,
And remember the legacy we leave.

Could it ever be a world without war?
Or will our children be left to grieve?

I think drugs are the scourge of our society. Creating vast problems worldwide. Our children need protecting and warning – 'Don't take the drugs'.

Don't Take the Drugs

Don't take the drugs.
Have a brilliant life while you can.
Live life to the full, but be careful.
Live a long life – but live like a man.

Don't take the drugs.
There's no need, life can be so sweet.
If you can stay strong, you'll find.
Drug dealers will beat a retreat.

Don't take the drugs.
You are worth much more than that.
We are none of us too weak to say.
No, to an evil fat cat.

Don't take the drugs.
All will be revealed one day.
Start at the beginning – you'll soon be win-
ning
There's a world without drugs – OK?

Don't take the drugs.
They make cowards of men.

Breathe the pure air of pleasure.
This much you owe your children.

I think the people who worked for Live Aid are wonderful. A charity worthy of the fantastic support it received.

Live Aid

It's an honour to support Live Aid,
It's a privilege to help this way.
If you've got limbs that work and eyes that see,
Can hear the birds each morn,
Consider those less fortunate
Without these gifts they're born.

If each day you wake – there's water
And food – however meagre.
You're warm enough and nearly well,
The elements not cruel, with enough sun for light.
Remember you are privileged.
Support the Live Aid plight.

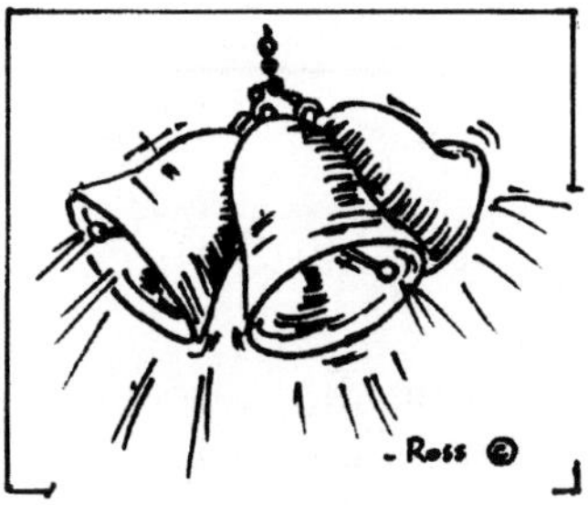

Wedding Fever

We're preparing for a wedding,
And fever's running high;
We've all got our new outfits,
Dad really needed a new tie!

The phone is like the hot-line,
Telecom's bonanza spree;
With all the interest stirred up,
We should get all our calls free!

Florist, cake and taxis,
To mention just a few;
Church and choir and organ,
All these services are due.

We've ordered lots of sunshine,
And given rain a rest;
We don't want splash and splatters,
For all must look their best.

It's nearly time for countdown,
Or in my case 'Out for the count';

We're really enjoying the panic,
What will we do when time runs out?

It's such a rush, I've hardly time
To write this little verse;
Help – I wish I'd not bothered,
I've only made things worse.

But jokes apart, and thoughts sincere,
I wouldn't change a minute;
With help from friends and families,
It seems the sky's the limit.

Pooled Effort

We're trying to strike it rich
On our Pools coupons this week,
We've pooled the office brains,
For we plan a winning streak.

We've juggled with the figures,
Checked birthdays past and present,
Even expected new deliveries
Are used in this event.

We've even counted fishes,
Our angling friends have caught,
But this unfortunately leaves us
With the rounded figure nought.

We've also studied ages
When big numbers we require,
But there's none to meet the Golf scores
Then figures go even higher.

We've even tried train numbers,
Or counting eggs our hens have laid.

Not one of our permutations,
Have so far made the grade.

But mark my words, we'll do it yet
The jackpot we'll hit with a clout,
And numbers won't matter a toss any more
Except when it comes to the Shareout.

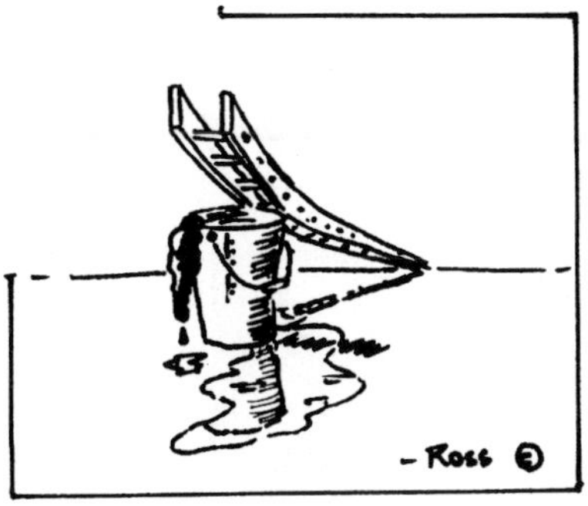

Our Window Cleaners

Different time, different days
They catch us on the hop.
We think we've got them sussed,
Then we see that we have not.

Got up early, curtains drawn,
I think the coast is clear.
Ready for the Full Monty now,
Oh no – the window cleaner's here!

Panic sets in, speed means all.
And I'm covered with confusion.
Husband shouts instructions, sharp.
To warn of this intrusion.

Ducking and diving with Bruno's skill
Is it curtains for me or the men?
Will my bubbles burst, but I fear the worst,
As I hold my breath and count to ten.

Steamed up windows, not just from the bath!
Have they gone, as I come up to breathe?

The ladder of life disappears from view.
As our window cleaners leave.

What a job they've got, and tales to tell.
Yet they really keep us on our toes.
Life would be boring for us and them.
Next chapter – nobody knows!

So if it's excitement you crave,
Then watch this space.
And see who will win,
In the window cleaners' race!

Big Frank's Day

I wrote this poem when Frank Bruno won his World Championship in 1995 and was awarded the MBE.

Our hearts go out to Frank –
Bruno, of course, I mean.
He was back on top form this weekend,
And says he's fulfilled his dream.

What a tower of strength he is,
With muscles on muscles galore.
Yet such a nice chap, you must agree.
And determined to come back for more.

'Unbelievable', his favourite word,
'You know what I mean?' he asks 'Arry.
He's in like a lion, and out like a lamb,
Only a fool would tarry.

He flew the flag for Britain,
The crowd helped his spirits soar.
'Unbelievable', his family and friends
  confirm,
As he says – he'll be back for more.

And if he moves in the right rings,
Sorry, *circles*, is what I should say.
We could perhaps hear 'Sir Frank' declare,
'It's unbelievable – I think I'll call it a day!'

Snow

Oh snow, you artist of magical scenes,
You lull us into false belief
That your wondrous snowscapes and frosted
  leaves
Are worlds away from grief.

Your skills enhance the winter dawn
Bring hush as your white cloak falls
As if by design, the bright sun shines,
And the birds cry of hunger calls.

As the peacock fans its feathers,
So you proudly display your wares,
Oh temptress with beguiling ways
Keep well hidden your secret snares.

Born Blind

Call him John or David or Paul
Seven years we have watched him
Groping in his darkness, knowing no better
Parents selected with precision
They are his guides and release from his
  prison.

  The patience they have shown seems
Not of this world but Heaven sent
Sculptors of each vision he sees
Every facet of his young life's experience
These gifts they endow for many years hence.

Already rewarded in various ways
  Their son, well adjusted and content
With his lot, two sisters to help
Share the load and balance in kind
None of them knowing why John was born
  blind.

I Wish I Could Sing

I wish I could sing
Instead of just croak.
Because, 'Give us a song',
Is really no joke!

I've got a Welsh name,
And ancestors too,
So why can't I sing,
Like they used to do?

Our school choir suffered,
With my added voice.
Perhaps, 'Gwyneth, recite a poem',
Would seem a wise choice!

I thought it seemed odd,
But our teacher looked fraught,
And mentioned 'Cats' chorus',
And the worst class she's taught!

I've done opera and pop,
Even jazz in the bath

To me – I sound brilliant,
But listeners just laugh!

Now, Karaoke's a nightmare,
I really can't win,
I'd sing along with pleasure,
But they won't let me in!

I wish I could sing,
Instead of just mime.
I don't believe what they tell me,
My voice is just fine.

I dream – I'll practice with the blackbirds,
And nightingales, if I must,
Then captivate my audience,
Who'll be spellbound and hushed!

But it's the real world we're in,
Where some can – and some can't,
So I'll settle for my poetry,
And see if that will enchant.

The Wrinkle

Got up this morning
What did I do?
I looked in the mirror
To see what was new.

It was there all right
Staring back at me.
A freshly made wrinkle
For all the world to see.

It must have waited
To catch me at low ebb.
Spotted the moment
Like a spider in its web.

I'll look again tomorrow
Recovered from the shock.
What's one little wrinkle?
I can't turn back the clock.

Tomorrow

I am to live in a luxurious home,
Palatial in fact, fit for a queen,
Gleaming paintwork, windows and gate
If I can but wait – Tomorrow.

Well kept lawns, paths, shrubs and trees.
Everything intact, neat and trim,
The knocker knocks, the door bell rings
Well, they will – Tomorrow.

All indoor decor spick and span
Cupboards will open, drawers will close.
Electrics working, yes washer and fridge.
If everything goes – Tomorrow.

The joiner will join, the plumber will plumb.
Not a trace of a squeak or a leak.
The clock that stopped when Grandad died
Once more will speak – Tomorrow.

Guess who is making these promises rare?
The love of my life, of course.
Who else but my husband will do all these things.
He will, you know – Tomorrow.

Shopping and Husbands

Shopping and husbands
Surely don't mix.
Avoiding the former
Is one of their tricks!

As long as all food
Is produced by thin air.
No questions asked
Just make sure it's there.

A table that groans
The gourmet's delight.
But don't ask them to shop –
They quickly take fright!

Too early to go
Too late to park up.
Complaints by the dozen.
The shops are full up!

Now clothes they're different.
He really blows his top

As he offers my wardrobe
To each fashion shop.

Shoes are no different.
No *more,* he'll plead.
He's now got the notion
I'm some centipede!

But all will change
If by chance he should meet
His long-lost friend
Or a pal in the street!

They talk boats or engines
With animated glee
While I watch and wait
For the next shopping spree!

My Cardboard Cut-out

I wouldn't say Graham was elusive,
But I've got a cardboard cut-out in case.
With all his coming and going,
I'm unable to recognise his face.

It sits at the table most evenings,
In an air that is tranquil and rare.
And there's no question of sport on the telly,
It's quite happy to sit there in the chair.

It's a most agreeable character,
Never talks about work or the like.
I don't even wash or cook for it,
It's almost like a sit-down strike.

But when it gets near to eleven,
And I hear Graham's car on the drive,
I pop it back in its box, pretty nifty,
And make way for the real 'Man Alive'.

Chill Out

Have you heard about the latest health tip?
It beats stretching and touching your toes.
Well – it's cold water baths or showers.
Until all your assets have froze!

It's supposed to do wonders for most folk.
By revvin' 'em up, like a car.
Makin' 'em 'ealthy and amazingly sprightly,
A kind of recovery service – five star!

Your body will tingle and glow,
Once you've plucked up the courage to try.
Just take it easy, drop by drop, is the answer.
I find a teaspoon, a good measure to go by!

They say it's good for your skin and complex-
ion,
And puts the sparkle back in your eyes.
You could even start running the marathon,
Or seek Olympic triumphs as your prize.

I believe there are benefits in other regions,
If you know what I mean – nod, nod, wink,
wink.

This is purely hearsay, believe me.
I've no personal experience of a link!

But don't take *my* word for it,
Save money on your heating bill.
Have an ice-cold shower or plunge.
I must go now – I've got a terrible chill!

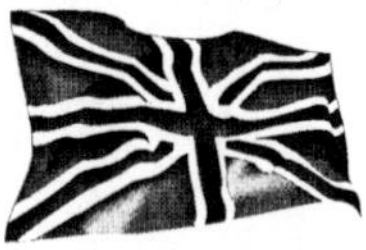

Britain

We are not able to turn the clock back.
It is no use living in the past.
We have a rapidly changing Britain,
Let's hope that good prevails and lasts.

We can do without the bad things,
With doom and gloom and war.
Let's brighten up and be thankful,
As Britain's great assets soar.

We have to live with change, like our fore-
bears.
Could they have imagined our world?
As new technology, knowing no limits,
And life changing knowledge unfurls.

Medical skills, once named 'Miracles',
Lighten our daily news.
More wonders than failures amaze us.
Help to show us which life we would choose.

Britain is still classed as 'Great', by me,
And if lessons of the past have been heeded,

Our country will shine like a beacon,
Lighting the dark side of life where needed.

The Power of Christmas

Christmas is so powerful,
Its magnetism so great.
Uniting people from far and wide,
Banishing hatred in its wake.

Children adore Christmas,
We adults take pleasure from this,
But the real reason for celebration,
Perhaps sometimes goes amiss.

Christmas can bring peace in war.
Enemies promise to cease-fire.
Then start again with bloodshed,
All hopes of peace expire.

God didn't send His son to us,
For love to be so short-lived.
We should observe the power of Christmas,
And treasure His ever-lasting gift.

Life As I Would Like To See It

A world of smiling faces,
A world of healing hands.
A wealth of understanding,
Throughout the wartorn lands.

Respect for fellow mankind,
And trust where there is doubt,
This is the world I would like to see,
With evil driven out.

And if this wish of mine comes true,
And enemies become good friends,
Life as I see it will be wonderful,
A future through rose-tinted lens.